Glyn Coy

Paul Timlett

Wiltshire is a long way from Lancashire, but it has been Glyn's home since 2006 when he decided a move to the country was in order, a place to raise his young family. Originally from the Liverpool area, Glyn spent a lot of his youth in North Wales where he developed a love of the countryside and long walks. While the mountains of Snowdonia and the rolling hills of Wiltshire are quite different, each has a beauty of their own.

Wiltshire has turned out to be the perfect place for Glyn to live, as a deep interest in ancient history and a love of photography work well together in the landscape here. The Hidden Wiltshire project is really a way to express those interests. Glyn is also behind all the aerial photography in the book.

A lifelong, if at times sporadic, passion for photography was finally fulfilled for Paul when he managed to engineer voluntary redundancy from a long and unsatisfying career in the finance sector in 2018. Since then he has been able to devote himself full time to his real love, interspersed with farming/ conservation work on a Natural England National Nature Reserve where he is a volunteer.

Originally from Sussex Paul has now lived in Wiltshire longer than he has lived anywhere else – 26 years. He photographs not just the landscape but seeks to document man's presence in it. As well as wide vistas he also photographs the small details which at times can be quite abstract. Paul also likes to travel for his photography, although Wiltshire remains his first love.

Glyn would like to dedicate this book to his sons Rohan, Luke and Jonah. He is hopeful that at least one of those sons will take over the mission one day. He would also like to thank his wife Daniela for her support and encouragement and Paul for seeing the vision and wanting to be part of it. Lastly, he would like to thank all of you who follow along. It is very much appreciated.

Paul would like to thank his long-suffering wife Julie for her support through his endeavours. He would also like to offer special thanks for the company of his walking buddy Stu, who has waited patiently whilst Paul fiddles with his camera on so many of the walks that have ended up as Hidden Wiltshire blogs. Where would we be without our hip flasks Stu? Last but not least he would like to thank Glyn for inviting him to participate in the Hidden Wiltshire project and this book in particular.

In this second Hidden Wiltshire book we continue our photographic journey through the most beautiful and ancient county of Wiltshire. During our travels we have developed a deep appreciation for these landscapes and a connection to those who have lived here before us.

Much of Wiltshire remains rural. Some of it is remote and wild. Long may it remain so. We hope this book inspires the reader to find their own Hidden Wiltshire.

Tan Hill

Looking across to Tan Hill, one of the highest hills in Wiltshire

Scaling the heights of Tan Hill on a sunny day in September, late summer sunflowers were still in bloom in the field at the bottom of the hill, which offered views to Bratton Camp in the distance. An old trailer in the field carried an archaic public health message to "Eat More Chips!".

A brisk walk followed, up the steep escarpment of Milk Hill to reach the plateau at the top of the Pewsey Downs, with the skies full of red kites and paragliders floating on the thermals.

The views from up here are among the finest you will see in Wiltshire, with Salisbury Plain to the South and Morgan's Hill to the West. Then followed a stroll along the Wansdyke before veering left to Tan Hill, from where the goal was to find Rybury Camp, a Neolithic causewayed enclosure and Iron Age hillfort guarded by a herd of Ruby Red cows from Bridge Farm.

Ruby red cows grazing on Rybury Camp

Eat More Chips

The medieval Wansdyke snakes its way across the Pewsey Vale, leaving Tan Hill behind. This intact stretch of dyke runs almost 14 miles from Marlborough to Morgan's Hill. The curiously named tree clump of Furze Knoll acts as a marker in this landscape. The Wansdyke travels in front of it, past the radio towers and down the hill in the distance.

Looking across to Milk Hill

Watching the harvest from the slopes of Tan Hill

Tinhead Long Barrow

Tinhead Hill and Long Barrow

Tinhead Hill today is mainly home to arable crops, woodland and an old farm which is now used for military training. But in the middle of a field, just below the natural summit of the hill, is this impressive tree clump that sits on top of a Neolithic long barrow.

As you walk up here and explore you see many curiosities. A manicured stretch of grass is actually an air strip for the aptly named Turnip Airways. If you time a walk right you might see aeroplanes land.

Walking along the byways that run across the hill will occasionally bring you face to face with military vehicles and the airspace is often shared with military helicopters or the occasional drone.

Turnip Airways - The Runway and Terminal Building

Tinhead Hill has one of twenty eight long barrows that exist on the Salisbury Plain Training Area, an area of special archaeological significance.

This particular barrow is sixty metres long, twenty nine metres wide and three metres high. Around fifteen metres of the length has been lost to ploughing. It was excavated in 1864 by John Thurnam who at the time was the medical superintendent of the Wiltshire county asylum at Devizes. He found that the barrow had been plundered before, but he did find traces of human remains and some Windmill Hill pottery.

TINHEAD HILL FARM

Picquet Hill and the Bottoms

Picquet Hill is a visually stunning location. It is surrounded by dry valleys such as Luccombe, Longcombe and Combe Bottom. These natural amphitheatres convey a sense of drama as the sun sets. On top of the hill is a stone bench, perfectly aligned to witness the disk of the sun setting against the western horizon.

Deep in the bowl of Luccombe Bottom, two hidden delights can be found. A solitary sarsen, known as the blood stone, is steeped in legend. Said to be an execution block used by King Alfred's army to remove the heads of the defeated Viking army after the Battle of Ethundun in 878, it has a subtle orange hue when the light of the sun catches it.

Further down in the valley is the gushing water of Luccombe spring. Here the chalk escarpment meets the clay, forcing water up to the surface which flows downhill forming the stream known as Stradbrook. During its time as the industrial heart of Bratton, this stream would have supported four textile mills.

Picquet Hill is one of those places that is rewarding to visit in all weathers. For a long time this solitary tree on the summit was a friend, offering itself up to be photographed. I tried for years to capture it from multiple angles, never being satisfied with the result.

But on a misty winter walk at the end of 2020 I got the photo I wanted. I'm glad I did, as the tree has now gone. Snapped at its base like a twig, probably due to a large cow with an itch to scratch, my photographic friend is no more. But there will always be other trees to find.

Folly Wood and the Headless Horseman

Folly Wood lies between Urchfont and Potterne. This sunken hollow that takes you through it is lined with trees where the gnarled roots cascade down the rock, giving rise to an almost gothic scene of horror. Next to the roots is a curious hole in the rock, the entrance to what is known as Holy Man's Cave.

An eccentric local gentleman called Seymour Wroughton owned a house on these lands known as Folly House. History has it that one night in 1789 Wroughton was drunk and recklessly drove his coach and horses home along this track. The coach overturned and Wroughton broke his neck. It is said that a headless horseman driving a coach and four still haunts the gorge.

The Deverills

The Deverills are a string of villages between Warminster and Mere.

This landscape is quintessential Wiltshire. Rolling green hills of chalk grassland play host to a Neolithic long barrow, a multitude of Bronze Age bowl barrows, Iron Age settlements, a Romano-Celtic temple, and the buried remains of a hugely significant Roman villa. The villages sit in a steep sided valley carved by the River Wylye, with hills above that reward exploration.

Cold Kitchen Hill to the left is home to the Neolithic long barrow as well as a Jubilee Beacon. From here you look towards Stourhead with Little Knoll rising up from the valley floor. The east side of Cold Kitchen Hill drops away to reveal Bushcombe Bottom and Bidcombe Hill. On the ridge can be seen Bidcombe Wood, home to a stunning display of bluebells and wild garlic each spring.

On the opposite side of the valley to Cold Kitchen Hill you will find Summerslade Down. The summit is home to a stone circle whose modernity has deceived many a historian. Nearby sits this beech clump, a favourite spot of a long deceased old farm worker whose ashes are scattered there. In early spring it is surrounded by daffodils but on this day it was surrounded by recently shorn sheep sheltering from the sun. I took their photograph – a timeless scene that could have been in the blistering heat of Greece.

Bidcombe Wood becomes a carpet of blue in the bluebell season. It is not easy to reach, with a steep climb from Kingston Deverill which deters all but the energetic visitor. There are many bluebell woods in Wiltshire that beg to be discovered but this one ranks as one of the best. For the photographer capturing the vibrancy of the colours is a challenge. Only a personal visit will do justice to the display.

A bold young fox rests on the gallops at Sutton Veny

Sutton Veny

St Leonard's Church, Sutton Veny

A rare example of a mortsafe

The village of Sutton Veny is a wonderful place to start a walk. Head south past the gallops and you will soon be up on Littlecombe Hill, with sweeping views across the Deverills to the south and the Warminster sky line to the north.

But the village itself is worthy of exploration. The church of St John on the high street is home to Commonwealth War Graves, many of whom were Australian soldiers who were victims of Spanish Flu in 1919.

The older abandoned St Leonard's Church has fallen into disrepair but you can still step inside the chancel. In the graveyard there is a curious mortsafe. I often wonder whether the family were genuinely concerned about body snatchers or were they just making a decorative statement?

Cold Kitchen Hill from Littlecombe Hill. The Neolithic long barrow lies just to the right of the summit

High above Sutton Veny, Littlecombe Hill and Bottom were active prehistoric sites. Bronze Age bowl barrows can be found near the top, while the remains of a Roman settlement can be found on nearby Tytherington Hill. The large wooded range of the Great Ridge is visible too, where its Roman road can still be walked as far as Lower Pertwood.

Kitt's Grave

Kitt's Grave is a liminal place where the parish boundaries of Bowerchalke and Ebbesbourne Wake meet, and the counties of Wiltshire, Dorset and Hampshire intersect. It is an ancient crossroads, once important and now mostly hidden by the ever expanding wood of Vernditch Chase. While marked on the map we never did find the elusive site of the grave.

Who was Kitt? We may never know for sure but there are different tales. A local gypsy woman? A girl from Bowerchalke who threw herself down a well? In the past, suicides were not buried in holy grounds and would often be laid to rest at a crossroads.

A place of great historical significance, the map marks two long barrows in the nearby woods. The Roman Ackling Dyke road runs to the south forming the border between Wiltshire and Hampshire. Various rights of way lead the curious to a multitude of barrows and earthworks on Marleycombe Hill looming above Bowerchalke and the Ebble Valley to the north.

Stone barn on Marleycombe Hill

Therein lies Kitt's Grave

Northwards from Marleycombe Hill

Marleycombe Hill looms over Bowerchalke

Robin Hood's Bower

Deep within the heart of Southleigh Wood is a prehistoric earthwork called Robin Hood's Bower. It is a sub-rectangular shape, marking an enclosure encircled by a ditch and bank.

It is a bizarre place covered in a discrete plantation of mature monkey puzzle trees. When approached in the dusky light of winter it feels like a dark place and can truly be described as spooky. Walk inside the Bower and you might spot evidence of strange rituals.

The wood itself is part of the Longleat Estate. The monkey puzzle plantation was planted in the 1960s on the instruction of the then Lord Weymouth, Alexander Thynn, later 7th Marquess of Bath.

There is a legend that the Bower was home to Iley Oak, and that King Alfred and his men rested here prior to the Battle of Ethundun in 878.

Codford Down

Codford Down is delightful in the summer. The bridleway that runs to the west of little Chitterne Brook is a beautiful and peaceful place. The area around the brook itself is rich in bird life, especially water fowl, whilst Red Kites quarter the skies above. It is also the gateway to trails heading west across Codford Down and Ansty Hill (another area worthy of exploration).

To the north can be seen the tumulus just south of Chitterne and an old fashioned water pump looking like something from the Mid-West of the United States.

Chitterne Brook is a winterbourne. In the winter months it flows well, but in the drier months of July and August it runs dry. Winterbournes generally form in areas where chalk downland gives way to clay, giving rise to springs.

Furze Knoll

an eerie place devoid of bird song

Wiltshire Clumps

Whilst not unique to Wiltshire, clumps are something that many of us envisage when we think of the county's landscape. These copses often comprise of beech trees planted in the 19th century to provide shelter or for ornamental purposes. They can be seen standing proud throughout the county, commanding all they survey.

Some of our clumps have become places of ceremony and it's not unusual to find offerings hanging from the trees. And it's not just humans who find these places attractive. A place for owls, buzzards and crows, their plaintive cries often the only disturbance to the whisper and scritch of the surrounding trees.

Sadly a lot of the beechwoods have reached maturity and are declining in health with landowners reluctant to go to the expense of maintaining or replacing them. It was sad to read in Robert Macfarlane's wonderful book "The Wild Places" that climate change means around 80-85% of our beech trees will disappear from Southern England by as soon as 2050 as they move north with the isobars, preferring a slightly cooler climate. Already many of our beeches have the appearance of trees hundreds of years older than their true age.

But as photographers, who can resist the sight of a beech clump standing majestically on the crown of a distant hill? Some of our favourites are included in the next few pages.

Copehill Down

On the 1:25,000 Ordnance Survey Map this clump is marked merely by a single tree symbol surrounded by a tiny blotch of green. But its position in the vast openness of chalk grassland is sufficiently elevated for it to be visible for great distances across the Plains in all directions, including to military transport aircraft whose pilots seem to use it as a navigational marker. In inclement weather it can be a wild, unforgiving place being exposed to all the elements can throw at it. It's not unusual to find owls and buzzards here. In mid-winter the icy blast of a strong northerly wind can make it feel arctic, especially in driven snow.

An arctic scene on Copehill Down

Old King Barrows is a simple clump, consisting of just four trees standing guard over a Bronze Age round barrow in the Stonehenge World Heritage Site. These four trees frequently keep their vigil alone, as most walkers pass them by to the west and head straight for the newer New King Barrows group, or plough the path to Stonehenge itself. Both barrow sites can be incorporated in an easy walk, perhaps from Woodhenge to Stonehenge, and a little time spent at the Old King Barrows will be rewarded with a view of this perfect little clump.

Old King Barrows

Oliver's Castle

The Iron Age hillfort of Oliver's Castle is an imposing sight for many miles around. The small number of trees on the summit have a commanding prominence, asserting themselves over the surrounding landscape.

Woodborough Hill

This is probably one of the most iconic of Wiltshire beech clumps, ever present to the gaze of the walker on the superior heights of Milk Hill and Tan Hill a short distance to the north. A whale's back of a hill with a copse perched on its summit, it is a photographer's dream as it stands in splendid isolation against the surrounding Vale of Pewsey.

Sadly the hill is surrounded almost entirely by private land reserved for the shoot. It can be approached by a single path alone that leads from the canal to its south, a quagmire in winter. This is a hill best admired from afar.

Great Ridge

Great Ridge is home to one of Wiltshire's largest woodlands. The spine of trees along the length of the ridge is visible for miles around, but this is an isolated wood which takes effort to reach.

While it may be an isolated place today, the course of a Roman road running through the centre, multiple ancient enclosures and a Grim's Ditch tell us that this was a place of great importance. Now a working wood and part of the Fonthill Estate, most of the people encountered here today are foresters. In years gone by local people had an ancient right to collect wood. It is also a place of rich and varied bird life where you may be privileged enough to hear the distinctive cry of the Goshawk or, if you are very lucky, catch a glimpse of one darting between trees.

It is possible to walk from the elevated summit of the wood down to the Wylye Valley through a multitude of bottoms.

In the distance, just above Corton, sits a Neolithic long barrow. Once the burial place of many ancient folks, today it looks down on the village and across to Knook and Heytesbury. How blessed we are to share this land with our ancestors.

On the opposite page a solitary, knarly oak marks the way on the Roman road by Snail-creep Hanging. This road can be traced all the way from Winchester, but is lost just beyond Great Ridge as it peters out by Lower Pertwood Farm.

The wood itself is an imposing sight in the landscape, stretching for well over three miles in length.

Top left: The spine of Great Ridge visible from Corton Down.

Bottom left: Corton Long Barrow.

Beckhampton Gallops

The Gallops at Beckhampton is an expanse of land with mixed use, split between racehorse training and agriculture. Its entirety can be seen from a northern ridgeway that rises up swiftly from the valley floor.

As with many areas in Wiltshire, it is filled with landscape markers of ancient history. A Roman road skirts the edge of the Gallops. Head north along it to Cherhill Down and Morgan's Hill or head south, which leads to Silbury Hill. The next page shows a view from the Roman road across to the Wansdyke, snaking its way up the hill towards the Pewsey Downs.

1917

Some of us photographers have been shooting this tree on Salisbury Plain for years. It stands out on the edge of the Imber Range, guarding the transition to the danger area. We call it the Lollipop Tree.

While it is easy to dismiss it as another unremarkable tree, once seen it almost comes alive. You start to spot it from many different places on the Plain and the Lollipop Tree becomes a visual anchor in the landscape.

The tree became a movie star not too long ago as it was the central point of the final scene in the World War One movie "1917". Indeed the whole field where this tree lives was converted for a few weeks into a film set, with trenches dug to replicate the wartime defensive structures in France. A fitting place to end this exploration of Hidden Wiltshire.

List of places visited in this book:

Tan Hill
Tinhead Hill
Picquet Hill
Folly Wood
The Deverills
Sutton Veny
Kitt's Grave
Robin Hood's Bower
Codford Down
Furze Knoll
Copehill Down
Old King Barrows
Oliver's Castle
Woodborough Hill
Great Ridge
Beckhampton Gallops
The Lollipop Tree

If you would like to continue to follow the Hidden Wiltshire journey, please visit the website at www.hiddenwiltshire.com. The site is regularly updated as we continue to explore and find new places to share and walks to follow.

A sign points the way along the Roman road from Beckhampton to Morgan's Hill